WOMEN WHO DARE

Women of the
Civil Rights Movement

BY LINDA BARRETT OSBORNE

Pomegranate
SAN FRANCISCO

LIBRARY OF CONGRESS
WASHINGTON, DC

Published by Pomegranate Communications, Inc.
Box 808022, Petaluma CA 94975
800 227 1428; www.pomegranate.com

Pomegranate Europe Ltd.
Unit 1, Heathcote Business Centre, Hurlbutt Road
Warwick, Warwickshire CV34 6TD, UK
[+44] 0 1926 430111; sales@pomeurope.co.uk

Amy Pastan, Series Editor

In association with the Library of Congress, Pomegranate publishes other books in the Women Who Dare® series, as well as calendars, books of postcards, posters, and Knowledge Cards® featuring daring women. Please contact the publisher for more information.

Library of Congress Cataloging-in-Publication Data

Osborne, Linda Barrett, 1949–
    Women of the civil rights movement / by Linda Barrett Osborne.
      p. cm. — (Women who dare)
    Includes bibliographical references.
    ISBN 0-7649-3548-8
    1. African Americans—Civil rights—History—20th century. 2. African American women civil rights workers—History—20th century. 3. Women civil rights workers—United States—History—20th century. 4. African American women civil rights workers—Biography. 5. Women civil rights workers—United States—Biography. 6. Civil rights movements—United States—History—20th century. 7. Women civil rights workers—United States—History—20th century—Pictorial works. 8. African Americans—Civil rights—History—20th century—Pictorial works. 9. Civil rights movements—United States—History—20th century—Pictorial works. I. Title. II. Women who dare (Petaluma, Calif.)

E185.61.O83 2006
323.082'0973—dc22

        2005049546

Pomegranate Catalog No. A114
Designed by Harrah Lord, Yellow House Studio, Rockport ME
Printed in Korea

15 14 13 12 11 10 09 08 07 06   10 9 8 7 6 5 4 3 2 1

FRONT COVER: The 1965 march from Selma to Montgomery, Alabama. LC-USZ62-133090
BACK COVER: Several of the "Little Rock Nine" students, protected by federal troops, arrive at Central High School. LC-U9-1054-E-9

PREFACE

FOR TWO HUNDRED YEARS, the Library of Congress, the oldest national cultural institution in the United States, has been gathering materials necessary to tell the stories of women in America. The last third of the twentieth century witnessed a great surge of popular and scholarly interest in women's studies and women's history that has led to an outpouring of works in many formats. Drawing on women's history resources in the collections of the Library of Congress, the Women Who Dare book series is designed to provide readers with an entertaining introduction to the life of a notable American woman or a significant topic in women's history.

From its beginnings in 1800 as a legislative library, the Library of Congress has grown into a national library that houses both a universal collection of knowledge and the mint record of American creativity. Congress' decision to purchase Thomas Jefferson's personal library to replace the books and maps burned during the British occupation in 1814 set the Congressional Library on the path of collecting with the breadth of Jefferson's interests. Not just American imprints were to be acquired, but foreign-language materials as well, and Jefferson's library already included works by American and European women.

The Library of Congress has some 121 million items, largely housed in closed stacks in three buildings on Capitol Hill that contain twenty public reading rooms. The incredible, wide-ranging collections include books, maps, prints, newspapers, broadsides, diaries, letters, posters, musical scores, photographs, audio and video recordings, and documents available only in digital formats. The Library serves first-time users and the most experienced researchers alike.

I hope that you, the reader, will seek and find in the pages of this book information that will further your understanding of women's history. In addition, I hope you will continue to explore the topic of this book in a library near you, in person at the Library of Congress, or by visiting the Library on the World Wide Web at http://www.loc.gov. Happy reading!

—JAMES H. BILLINGTON, The Librarian of Congress

■ *Mass meetings were the lifeblood of the civil rights movement, and women often made up a majority of the audience. Frequently held at churches, where speakers encouraged, inspired, and exhorted people to action, such meetings rallied entire communities to participate in marches, demonstrations, and voter registration drives. Here, women attend a meeting at the Shiloh Baptist Church in Albany, Georgia, in August 1962.*

WOMEN OF THE
CIVIL RIGHTS MOVEMENT

I think that the work the women did during the time of civil rights is what really carried the movement along. The women carried forth the ideas. I think the civil rights movement would never have taken off if some women hadn't started to speak up.

—Septima Clark
Teacher, activist, and organizer of citizenship schools

If Mrs. Parks had got up and given that white man her seat you'd never a heard of Reverend King.

—Edgar Daniel (E. D.) Nixon
Head of the Montgomery, Alabama NAACP

They are captured forever in the photographs and film footage that document the civil rights movement of the 1950s and 1960s: women walk to their jobs in Montgomery, Alabama, as the buses roll by, unoccupied; women sit in at lunch counters, unserved, while white crowds jeer; women line the pews at mass meetings that fill churches to overflowing, or defend themselves from the spray of fire hoses and climb into paddy wagons. Women move in peaceful protest down the broad streets of Washington, DC, and they march the fifty-four miles from Montgomery to Selma, Alabama.

■ *The civil rights movement of the 1950s and 1960s focused on ending legal segregation in the eleven states of the former Confederacy and in Oklahoma, Missouri, Kentucky, West Virginia, Maryland, Delaware, and the District of Columbia. "White only" signs, such as this one on a vending machine, were the visible symbols of segregation.*
LC-USZ62-116815

Women are in the pictures, but they are not at the podiums. Men assumed most of the media-friendly, highly visible leadership roles at marches and rallies, yet women did far more than swell the ranks of civil rights demonstrators. Although they were often neglected in the press at the time, and later in history texts, women initiated action, headed organizations, and made tough decisions. They were at the forefront in planning for—and precipitating—the pivotal events of the time. Rosa Parks refused

■ *Schools, housing, libraries, restaurants, parks and beaches, and theaters, like the one shown here in Leland, Mississippi, in 1937, were segregated. If a theater were open to both whites and African Americans, African Americans were forced to sit in the balcony.*
LC-USF34-17417

to give up her seat on a Montgomery, Alabama, bus, inspiring mass action against segregation; Jo Ann Gibson Robinson started the boycott of Montgomery's buses by blanketing the city with flyers the morning after Parks' arrest; Ella Baker was the first person to run the Southern Christian Leadership Conference (SCLC) and to bring together the students who formed the Student Nonviolent Coordinating Committee (SNCC); Daisy Bates kept the "Little Rock Nine" in Central High School; Diane Nash rallied the Freedom Riders when racist violence threatened to stop them in their tracks.

8

■ *A church service in Woolville, Greene County, Georgia, in October 1941. Churches became prominent meeting places during the civil rights movement, and church women, often dressed in their Sunday best, participated en masse in voter registration campaigns, marches, and demonstrations.* LC-USF34-46153-D

■ *Transportation was also segregated: African Americans were expected to sit in the backs of buses or in designated railway cars. The sign in this photograph points travelers toward the "white waiting room" at a Greyhound bus terminal in Memphis, Tennessee, in September 1943.* LC-USW3-37974-E

■ *African American women, as well as men, served in the armed forces during World War II. These US Army nurses—Joan L. Hamilton, Geneva Culpepper, Marjorie S. Mayers, Prudence L. Burnes, and Inez E. Holmes—were stationed in Australia in 1944. When veterans returned to the United States, they were reluctant to resume life under segregation.* LC-USZ62-94040

FOCUS ON SEGREGATION

THE MODERN CIVIL RIGHTS movement embraced post–World War II efforts to end legalized segregation. After serving in the war, black Americans came home to towns and cities where they had to drink from "colored only" water fountains or sit at the backs of buses simply because of the color of their skin. Those who intended to dismantle segregation followed two main strategies. One approach challenged segregation laws and practices through the courts, with the ultimate goal of overturning the

■ *Mabel Staupers (left), shown here with civil rights activist Lillian Smith, was the longtime executive secretary of the National Association of Colored Graduate Nurses. Staupers (1890–1989) successfully campaigned for the US Army to eliminate its quota system for black nurses in 1945, and for the navy to begin recruiting black nurses.*
LC-USZ62-118829

1896 Supreme Court decision *Plessy v. Ferguson*, which mandated "separate but equal" public accommodations. The other mobilized large numbers of people for peaceful mass protests and demonstrations.

During the 1940s, women were involved in every aspect of the civil rights movement. Constance Baker Motley, hired in 1946 as an attorney for the National Association for the Advancement of Colored People's Legal Defense Fund, helped to prepare the briefs for the landmark Supreme Court decision *Brown v. Board of Education*. Daisy Lampkin, a national field secretary for the NAACP who simultaneously worked with the National Association of Colored Women and the National Council of Negro Women, was an extraordinarily able fund-raiser and membership recruiter who built mass support among black workers.

Ella Baker, an outstanding grassroots organizer who joined the NAACP as a field secretary in 1940 and served as director of branches from 1943 to 1946, emphasized the importance and power of mass participation as a vehicle for achieving civil rights. Ruby Hurley assumed the role of NAACP national youth secretary in 1943; during her tenure, she more than tripled the number of youth councils and college chapters (to 280). These women excelled at raising the organization's membership levels, which had dropped during the Great Depression, and at pressing conservative male leaders into more assertive action. They consistently voiced women's concerns and advocated placing women in leadership positions.

Women also made contributions outside the framework of the NAACP. In the mid-1940s, Pauli Murray led sit-ins at drugstores and cafeterias—some fifteen years before sit-ins became a national phenomenon—

■ *Daisy Lampkin (c. 1884–1965) campaigned for women's suffrage before she joined the NAACP staff in 1930. She was also the vice president of the company that published the* Pittsburgh Courier, *an influential black newspaper that gave her an added venue for promoting her many antilynching and fundraising campaigns. Here, Lampkin holds a sign articulating the "Double V" strategy of black Americans during World War II: to work for victory against fascism overseas and victory against racial injustice at home.*

LC-USZ62-119472

while studying law at Howard University in Washington, DC. There she encountered the prevalent bias against professional women: "I entered law school preoccupied with the racial struggle . . . but I graduated an unabashed feminist as well," she said later. She also graduated first in her class.

■ *Women made up a large part of the NAACP's membership. As paid staff or volunteers, they were also active and highly successful in attracting new members. This photograph shows a sidewalk recruiting station attended by three women in New York City in 1961.*

■ *Ella Baker recruited members, raised funds, and supported local programs and campaigns for the NAACP in the early years of her career. Fiercely independent, Baker (1903–1986) believed in democratic grassroots activism that stressed the role of many ordinary people rather than individual leaders in achieving social and political change. "Strong people," she declared, "don't need strong leaders."* LC-USZ62-110575

■ *In 1951, Ruby Hurley (b. 1913) opened the first permanent NAACP office in the Deep South, in Birmingham, Alabama, where she investigated lynchings and supported Autherine Lucy Foster's bid to enter the all-white University of Alabama. "I could be riding down the street and white men would drive by and say, 'We gon' get you,'" she recalled. "Bombs were thrown at my home."* LOOK MAGAZINE COLLECTION. LC-L9-57-7241-FF #15

■ *NAACP attorney Constance Baker Motley argued ten cases before the Supreme Court, and won nine. She was one of the lawyers for Autherine Lucy Foster in her attempt to integrate the University of Alabama, and was the attorney for James Meredith, who became the first African American to attend the University of Mississippi. In 1966, Motley (1921–2005) became the first African American woman to be appointed a federal district judge.* LC-USZ62-122141

■ *Pauli Murray (1910–1985), a graduate of Hunter College and Howard University Law School, became an early Freedom Rider when she was arrested in Petersburg, Virginia, for "disorderly conduct"—refusing to accept the segregation of interstate bus passengers. After she was convicted, she chose to stay in jail rather than pay her fine, in the tradition of nonviolent protest.* LC-USZ62-109644

Murray found a mentor in Lillian Smith, a liberal white Southerner who defied every convention of her time and place, holding interracial gatherings at her mountaintop home in northern Georgia. Smith published the literary journal *South Today*, which printed fiction and articles by black and white writers, and she freely denounced racial prejudice and its

■ *Lillian Smith (1897–1966) spoke and wrote widely on behalf of political and social equality for blacks and whites. Among her most provocative works were* Strange Fruit, *a tragic novel about an interracial love affair, and* Killers of the Dream, *a nonfiction work exploring the impact of racial prejudice and the system of segregation on both blacks and whites.* LC-USZ62-109699

place in white culture. She was particularly outspoken and brave, but she was not alone among white women in protesting against the treatment of African Americans. In 1930 Jessie Ames was one of a group who founded the Association of Southern Women for the Prevention of Lynching, which had more than 40,000 members in the early 1940s.

■ *Social worker Mary White Ovington (fourth from right) was a founder of the NAACP. She is shown here with other NAACP luminaries, including W. E. B. Du Bois (third from right).* LC-USC62-5805

A LEGACY OF ACTIVISM

WOMEN'S RESISTANCE to racial inequality, injustice, and discrimination has existed for as long as has the institution of slavery: think of abolitionists Harriet Tubman and Sojourner Truth. These nineteenth-century heroines were followed by turn-of-the-century activists such as Ida B. Wells, who led a fiery campaign against lynching, and Mary Church Terrell, founder of the National Association of Colored Women.

Wells and Terrell were two of some twenty women (there were sixty people altogether) who cofounded the NAACP in 1909. Another founder, Mary White Ovington, a white social worker who supported black and female leadership roles in the organization, was the NAACP's board chairman in the 1920s and assumed the job of treasurer in 1932.

Women formed a significant part of the NAACP's early membership. Already involved in social and political activism through black women's clubs, they were eager to participate in activities aimed at ending discrimination and racial violence. Mary Talbert, a veteran clubwoman from Buffalo, New York, recruited an impressive number of these members. In 1918 she became the NAACP's vice president and national director of its key program, an antilynching campaign.

Daring and influential, women like Wells, Terrell, Talbert, and Ovington shaped the civil rights movement and set the stage for the generations to come. ■

■ *Mamie Till-Mobley, whose fourteen-year-old son, Emmett, was murdered in Mississippi, falls to her knees as the train bearing her son's body arrives in Chicago. Till-Mobley (1922–2003) courageously transformed the tragedy of her son's death into a force for change, touring the country on behalf of the NAACP. "The murder of my son has shown me that what happens to any of us, anywhere in the world, had better be the business of us all," she concluded.* LC-USZ62-118182

FROM THE SUPREME COURT TO MONTGOMERY, ALABAMA

THE 1950S WITNESSED a major breakthrough in the fight against segregation. The Supreme Court's 1954 decision in *Brown v. Board of Education* rejected *Plessy v. Ferguson*'s "separate but equal" doctrine and concluded that "separate educational facilities are inherently unequal." It called for public schools to be integrated.

Brown v. Board of Education addressed five school desegregation cases heard together by the court. One of these was *Davis v. County School Board of Prince Edward County*, an action initiated by sixteen-year-old Barbara Johns, a junior at Moton High School in rural Farmville, Virginia. Johns' school was too small for its 450 African American students, so tarpaper-and-wood shacks had been built to hold the overflow. When, in 1951, the white school board refused to build a new school, Johns led her classmates in a boycott. She also called in the NAACP, which, after some negotiation, accepted the students' case against Prince Edward County. Johns left Virginia to maintain her safety.

Another teenager made the news in 1955, in one of the most tragic events of the civil rights movement. Fourteen-year-old Emmett Till was murdered after flirting mildly with a white woman in Money, Mississippi. When his mutilated body was returned to his home in Chicago, and his mother, Mamie Till-Mobley, saw how badly disfigured her son was, she insisted that "the whole world . . . see what I had seen." There was little precedent for black families publicizing racially motivated killing, but Till-Mobley held an open-casket funeral and the press picked up Emmett's story. The white men accused of the crime were acquitted, but Till-Mobley, determined to expose the horror of lynching in the South, had made her point.

Three months later, Rosa Parks made *her* point when she refused to give up her bus seat to a white man, on December 1, 1955. Parks, who was secretary of the Montgomery branch of the NAACP and adviser to the NAACP Youth Council, precipitated the Montgomery bus boycott of 1956–1957. She later wrote: "People always say that I didn't give up my seat because I was tired, but that isn't true. I was not tired physically, or no more tired than I usually was at the end of a working day. I was not old, although some people have an image of me as being old then. I was forty-two. No, the only tired I was, was tired of giving in."

Parks stayed in her seat, but it was Jo Ann Gibson Robinson, an English professor at Alabama State College and president of the Women's Political Council (WPC) of Montgomery, who initiated the boycott. She had suggested the tactic earlier; when she heard about Parks' arrest, she surreptitiously mimeographed 35,000 flyers in the dead of night, requesting blacks to boycott Montgomery's buses on the day of Parks' trial. WPC workers distributed them throughout the city. The bus boycott, the movement's first mass action of the 1950s, drew support from Virginia Durr, another prominent Montgomery civil rights advocate. A white Southerner and founder of the Southern Conference for Human Welfare, Durr was ostracized in Alabama for her friendship and efforts on behalf of African Americans.

In the wake of the boycott, Martin Luther King Jr. and other black male ministers founded the Southern Christian Leadership Conference (SCLC) in

■ *Rosa Parks had attended the Highlander Folk School, a training center for labor and civil rights leadership, just months before she was arrested and fined $10 for violating Montgomery's segregation laws. Three months after the incident, she was one of eighty-nine African Americans arrested under a 1921 law prohibiting boycotts. In this photograph Parks (1913–2005) is being fingerprinted by Deputy Sheriff D. H. Lackey in the Montgomery jail on February 22, 1956, for breaking the boycott law.*

■ *As early as 1920, Septima Clark (1898–1987) successfully campaigned to permit African Americans to teach in the city of Charleston's schools, and later, for equal pay for black and white teachers. In 1956, after forty years in the South Carolina school system, she was fired for refusing to give up her NAACP membership. She then commenced her "second career," establishing citizenship schools. In this photograph, Clark (center) is leading a class on Johns Island, South Carolina, in 1959.* PHOTOGRAPH © IDA BERMAN

1957. They proposed a voter registration campaign, but no one stepped forward to organize it until a woman, Ella Baker, agreed to coordinate the campaign. She also established the SCLC office. Although Baker was named the organization's acting director, and later acting executive director, the board

■ *Jo Ann Gibson Robinson (1912–1992), who printed and distributed flyers calling for a bus boycott, became a quiet but essential player in the Montgomery Improvement Association, the group that directed the boycott. Subjected to threats and violence, she once described her acid-damaged Chrysler with pride: "It had become the most beautiful car in the world to me."*

never recognized her work with a permanent title. "The basic attitude of men and especially ministers, as to . . . the role of women in their church setups, is that of taking orders, not providing leadership," Baker declared; the attitude persisted in the administration of civil rights organizations.

Another woman, Septima Clark, became involved with the SCLC in 1959, recruiting African Americans to participate in a program that taught basic literacy and citizenship skills. Clark had pioneered the idea of citizenship schools at the Highlander Folk School in the 1950s: "I just thought that you couldn't get people to register and vote until you could teach them to read and write," she explained. Through her efforts, 897 citizenship schools were organized by 1970. Clark, too, later expressed her frustration at the way male SCLC members treated her. "I was just a figurehead. . . . Whenever I had anything to say, I would put up my hand and say it. But I did know that they weren't paying attention." They were, however, willing for her to do the time-consuming, hard work of grassroots organizing, outside the limelight, and she made a difference. Her citizenship schools had a significant impact on black political participation after passage of the 1965 Voting Rights Act.

TOPPLING SEGREGATED EDUCATION

SCHOOL DESEGREGATION continued to be an issue even after the *Brown* decision, and women played a critical part in its implementation. In 1956, six years before James Meredith famously integrated the then all-white University of Mississippi, Authorine Lucy Foster became the first African American to enroll at the University of Alabama. Foster had asked the NAACP to go to court to win her acceptance. She enrolled as a graduate student in library science on February 3; three days after she started classes, mobs threatened her life. The university suspended Foster for what they claimed was her own safety, and after a court appeal failed, she was expelled. Her experience underlined the difficulty in achieving integration even when it was mandated by law.

Perhaps the best-known attempt to integrate a school took place in Little Rock, Arkansas, in 1957, when white mobs prevented nine black students chosen to integrate Central High School from entering. Six of the "Little Rock Nine" were young women: Minnijean Brown, Elizabeth Eckford, Thelma Mothershed, Melba Patillo, Gloria Ray, and Carlotta Walls. Again, a woman took the lead in organizing and supporting the students: Daisy Bates, president of the Arkansas NAACP. Bates endured constant harassment, and a rock was thrown through her window with the scribbled message "Stone this time, dynamite next" attached to it; her home was bombed later that year. Yet Bates would not give in to the threats. The students credited her courage for enabling them to make it through the school year. ■

■ *Thurgood Marshall and Arthur Shores (center and right foreground) served, along with Constance Baker Motley, as attorneys for Autherine Lucy Foster (left foreground) in her bid to attend the University of Alabama. Demonstrations led to her expulsion. In 1989 Foster (b. 1929) reenrolled at the university, earning an MA in elementary education at the same time that her daughter Grazia received her bachelor's degree from Alabama.*

LC-USZ62-108276. COURTESY AP/WIDE WORLD

■ *On February 6, 1956, white mobs demonstrated against the enrollment of Autherine Lucy Foster at the University of Alabama. In this photograph, students are shown burning literature about desegregation and waving Confederate flags. Mobs such as this one harassed civil rights activists, disrupted sit-ins and marches, and prevented African American students from integrating schools and universities.* LC-USZ62-120216

■ *Little Rock, Arkansas, was a relatively liberal community that had agreed to desegregate schools in compliance with* Brown v. Board of Education. *Just before school opened in 1957, however, Governor Orval Faubus announced that he would call out the Arkansas National Guard to "maintain order" in case of "forcible integration." President Dwight Eisenhower had to send in federal troops to protect the nine students who integrated the school, including the ones shown here.* LC-U9-1054-E-9

■ *Daisy Bates (1922–1999) organized and protected the "Little Rock Nine" who desegregated Central High School in 1957. Bates and her husband also owned the* Arkansas State Press, *a weekly newspaper that spoke out against racial discrimination. When the NAACP planned to bestow the Spingarn Medal, its highest award, on the "Little Rock Nine," the students refused to accept the medal unless Bates was included as a recipient.* LC-USZ62-115050

■ *Known for her integrity and coolness under fire, Diane Nash (second from right) was a leader of the sit-in movement who later worked for the SCLC. In 1962, Nash (b. 1938) was convicted of "contributing to the delinquency of minors" when she recruited teenagers for civil rights demonstrations. She was also pregnant, and told the judge she would have her baby in jail. "This will be a black baby born in Mississippi, and thus wherever he is born, he will be in prison," she said. Nash was released without serving a sentence.*

PHOTOGRAPH COURTESY *THE TENNESSEAN*

THE 1960S: SIT-INS, PICKET LINES, AND MASS DEMONSTRATIONS

THE 1960S KICKED OFF with a legendary event of the civil rights movement. On February 1, four black students sat in at a Woolworth's lunch counter in Greensboro, North Carolina. Within weeks, lunch counter sit-ins were taking place throughout the South—as well as kneel-ins at all-white churches, wade-ins at swimming pools, and picket lines in front of movie theaters and department stores. Many of the protesters were students trained in nonviolent strategy. They learned to sit patiently while crowds harassed them, sometimes pelting them with food or pulling them from their seats. Diane Nash, a student at Fisk University, became a leader of the sit-ins that resulted in the desegregation of lunch counters in Nashville, Tennessee. She was also a founding member of the Student Nonviolent Coordinating Committee.

Ella Baker of the SCLC called together the students who formed SNCC, advising them to maintain their independence from established civil rights groups. SNCC members formed the front lines of nonviolent confrontation, risking attacks and arrests as they organized voter registration drives, sit-ins, and antisegregation demonstrations, often in small towns and without major publicity.

Both black and white students worked for SNCC, and an impressive number of members were women. Baker believed in "group-centered leadership," rather than in a hierarchical organization with an individual leader; her approach, embraced by the students, encouraged women to

■ *In 1960, Ella Baker called for a student conference that led to the formation of the Student Nonviolent Coordinating Committee. Baker was the organization's mentor and fervent supporter, but she was not its leader: "The whole is greater than the part," she believed. "That is the concept of developing a movement that involves people to the extent that they become knowledgeable about their own condition and . . . activated to do something about it."* PHOTOGRAPH © DANNY LYON/MAGNUM

take active roles. Jane Stembridge, Dorie and Joyce Ladner, June Johnson, Bernice Reagon, Dottie Miller, Casey Hayden, Judy Richardson, and Ruby Doris Smith were among those who faced beatings and jail time to end segregation. Many of them practiced a "jail-no-bail" policy, refusing release in order to fill prisons to overflowing so that their presence could not be ignored, and whites would be forced to face the seriousness of the students' commitment.

Women signed up for the Freedom Rides in 1961, when CORE—the Congress of Racial Equality—organized black riders to sit in the front seats of buses and white riders to sit in the back. The goal was to test whether southern states were obeying a federal order that prohibited the segregation of interstate buses, bus stations, and restaurants. The first two buses left Washington, DC, on May 4; in Anniston, Alabama, a white mob set fire to one bus, and another mob beat the Freedom Riders from the second bus as police looked on. CORE was ready to abandon the effort, but Diane Nash jumped in. She quickly organized SNCC students to replace the riders and inspired CORE members to return to the rides as well. Because of Nash, hundreds of volunteers rode Freedom buses throughout the summer.

Like Ella Baker, Nash seemed to play a critical part at every stage of the movement. As an organizer for the SCLC in 1962 and 1963, she was instrumental in conceiving the long-term strategy that led to the 1963 March on Washington and to the Selma, Alabama, voting rights campaign. She also participated in the 1963 campaign against segregation in Birmingham, Alabama—a turning point in the movement. Eugene "Bull"

■ *Diane Nash rallied SNCC and CORE members to resume the Freedom Rides after the first two buses were attacked. This photograph shows the bus bombed outside Anniston, Alabama. A female Freedom Rider sits in near collapse on the ground. At one point, National Guardsmen were called in to escort the buses, which continued to roll all summer.* LC-USZ62-118472

Connor, the city safety commissioner, responded to the first protesters with arrests, and soon with police dogs and high-pressure fire hoses. Schoolgirls as young as six were hauled into paddy wagons. So many

■ *In 1963, the SCLC led a protest against segregation in Birmingham, Alabama. In this photograph, three protesters hold fast against a blast of water strong enough to tear the bark off trees.* PHOTOGRAPH © BETTMAN/CORBIS

young people were arrested that the Birmingham campaign became known as the Children's Crusade. Television captured these scenes, providing a wide audience with its first look at the violence underlying segregation.

NONVIOLENT RESISTANCE

Advocated by Mahatma Mohandas Gandhi during the quest for India's independence, and by Martin Luther King Jr. and the early members of SNCC, passive resistance was a powerful technique used by civil rights demonstrators. Protesters were trained to sit patiently while crowds harassed them, sometimes pelting them with food, pulling them from lunch-counter seats, or beating or kicking them.

Those who practiced nonviolent resistance were willing to be arrested for acts of civil disobedience, such as blocking traffic or refusing to disperse from public places. They went limp as police carried them to paddy wagons. It took tremendous courage to remain peaceful and courteous as violence was directed against them by crowds and police. ■

■ *During a 1963 civil rights demonstration in Brooklyn, New York, an unidentified woman is carried to a paddy wagon by police.* LC-USZ62-134715

■ One of tens of thousands of women who participated in civil rights demonstrations, *Ruth Tinsley, shown here, refused to leave a picket line outside a department store in Richmond, Virginia, on February 24, 1960. Like other nonviolent protestors—who would not retaliate with violence themselves, but who also would not abandon their places—she was dragged away from the scene by two policemen.* LC-USZ62-119523

■ *These teenaged girls were imprisoned for nine days in a stockade near Leesburg, Georgia, after taking part in a civil rights demonstration. "There were thirty-two kids in there with me," said Lois Barnum Holley, one of the prisoners, in an affidavit. "There were no beds, no mattresses, no blankets, pillows, no sheets. The floor was cold. You lay down for while and soon it starts hurting . . . so you have to walk around for a while."*

PHOTOGRAPH © DANNY LYON/MAGNUM

■ *Sit-ins were a staple of the civil rights movement, and many of the participants were students. Trained in nonviolent strategy, they learned to sit patiently while white crowds harassed them or tried to pull them from their seats. In this photograph demonstrators— many of them SNCC members, including Joyce Ladner (center)—sit in at a Toddle House restaurant in Atlanta during the winter of 1963–1964.* PHOTOGRAPH © DANNY LYON/MAGNUM

■ *On June 10, 1963, in Danville, Virginia, police attacked demonstrators praying for an end to segregation. SNCC member Dottie Miller was one of forty-eight people injured. In this photograph, she describes her experience to James Forman, SNCC's executive director. She is barefoot, since her shoes were lost when she was sprayed with fire hoses. She was also clubbed.*

PHOTOGRAPH © DANNY LYON/MAGNUM

■ *"We live in a town where a man might be killed tomorrow, where civil war might break out next week," said Gloria Richardson (b. 1922), shown here (center) in police custody in Cambridge, Maryland. "It cannot get better while the white people fail to understand the mood of the Negro community and to realize that unless they grant the means of progress, their houses and ours may fly apart."*

PHOTOGRAPH © DANNY LYON/MAGNUM

A WATERSHED YEAR

THE YEAR 1963 proved extraordinary. As demonstrators marched in Birmingham, Gloria Richardson, co-chair of the Cambridge Nonviolent Action Committee, led a protest campaign in Cambridge, Maryland. The demonstrators' demands went beyond desegregation of public accommodations and included school integration, fair job policies, and public housing. Dozens of people were arrested, the National Guard was called in to quell violence, and Richardson met with Attorney General Robert Kennedy, but no solution was reached. Although she was criticized for not compromising, Richardson broached issues ahead of their time; by the late 1960s her view—attacking the broader aspects of discrimination, not just legal segregation—would be widely shared.

As the year progressed, a committee planned the March on Washington, scheduled for the end of August. There were nineteen members on the committee; eighteen were men. The sole woman, Anna Hedgeman, was a community activist who had worked for New York City's mayor and run for political office. The men accepted Hedgeman's suggestion that the goal of the march be "jobs and freedom" as well as civil rights legislation, but they were unconcerned when she protested the fact that no woman was planned to be a key speaker. Without Hedgeman, there would not have been even a short "Tribute to Women" hastily added to the program. On August 28, when the march took place, women filled the streets of Washington, DC, but no women marched in the lead or spoke at the Lincoln Memorial. That lapse was as symbolic of the status of women in the civil rights movement as the march itself was a testament to the progress that had been made.

■ *Tens of thousands of women attended the March on Washington on August 28, 1963. Drawing an estimated 250,000 people, it was the largest demonstration up to that time in the United States. Mahalia Jackson and Marian Anderson sang, but no women participated as major speakers.* LC-U9-10364-37 (above); LC-U9-10358 (right)

■ *Four fourteen-year-old girls were killed when a bomb set by the Ku Klux Klan exploded in the Sixteenth Street Baptist Church in Birmingham, Alabama, on September 11, 1963. On the day of their funeral, a grieving crowd lined the route of the funeral procession. This photograph shows SNCC members Dorie Ladner (holding flag), Dona Richards, and Doris Derby, with Sam Shirah standing behind Richards.*

PHOTOGRAPH © DANNY LYON/MAGNUM

■ *Sharecropper Fannie Lou Hamer worked with SNCC, dedicating herself to voter registration. When a reporter asked if she were trying to be equal with a white man, she replied: "I don't want to go down that low. I want the true democracy that'll raise me and that white man up . . . raise America up." In this photograph, Hamer (1917–1977) marches in a 1964 demonstration in Hattiesburg, Mississippi.*
PHOTOGRAPH © DANNY
LYON/MAGNUM

Two weeks after the March on Washington, a bomb put in place by the Ku Klux Klan exploded inside Birmingham's Sixteenth Street Baptist Church. Twenty-one children were injured, and four fourteen-year-olds died: Addie Mae Collins, Denise McNair, Carole Robertson, and Cynthia Wesley. Despite shock and outrage, the city remained quiet and the day of the girls' funeral was peaceful.

THE RIGHT TO VOTE

NEARLY A YEAR after the March on Washington, President Lyndon Johnson signed the Civil Rights Act into law on July 2, 1964. The law banned segregation in public accommodations; it also reaffirmed the right of every American to vote. But southern states continued to use obstructive tactics to keep African Americans away from the polls, and to address this problem, SNCC organized "Freedom Summer" in Mississippi. Student volunteers, many of them women, worked to educate and register black voters, to provide access to health care and legal aid, and to build support for the Mississippi Freedom Democratic Party (MFDP), an independent political entity set up to challenge the state's all-white Democratic Party.

Eighty thousand African Americans joined the MFDP. The party sent elected representatives to the 1964 Democratic National Convention, where the Democratic candidate for president would be nominated. These representatives asked to be seated as Mississippi's rightful delegates, since blacks had been excluded from choosing the all-white delegation. To persuade the committee to seat them, Fannie Lou Hamer, co-chair of the MFDP, described an experience after she was arrested for

■ *The 1965 march from Selma to Montgomery, Alabama, took place over four days and covered fifty-four miles. Nearly thirty thousand people joined in for the final three-mile stretch. The Selma campaign focused national attention on the issue of voting rights, leading to passage of the Voting Rights Act of 1965.* LC-USZ62-133090

attending a civil rights meeting. "They beat me and they beat me with the long, flat blackjack," she recounted on national television. "I screamed to God in pain. My dress worked itself up. I tried to pull it down. They beat my arms till I had no feeling in them." Despite Hamer's eloquence, the MFDP delegates were offered only two seats at the convention; they

■ *A thirty-nine-year-old mother of five children, Viola Liuzzo was a part-time student at Detroit's Wayne State University who had already participated in civil rights protests. When she saw the televised attack by state troopers on the peaceful marchers heading from Selma to Montgomery, Liuzzo felt compelled to drive her green Oldsmobile for three straight days to join the demonstrations. On March 25, she was murdered by Ku Klux Klansmen.* LIBRARY OF CONGRESS, GENERAL COLLECTIONS

■ *An activist since her student days at Spelman College, Marian Wright Edelman was the first African American woman to pass the bar examination in Mississippi. Edelman (b. 1939) worked as an attorney to defend civil rights advocates and to integrate schools.*

refused the compromise. Thanks to Hamer, however, they succeeded in showcasing their cause.

Like the MFDP, the 1965 march from Selma, Alabama, to the state capital, Montgomery, drew attention to voting inequities. The Selma demonstrators began by marching to the courthouse several times, and many were arrested. On March 7, six hundred demonstrators tried to cross the Edmund Pettus Bridge on their way to Montgomery; they were beaten and dispersed by helmeted Alabama state troopers on horseback. The march resumed on March 21, guarded by federal troops. Viola Liuzzo, a housewife from Detroit, was ferrying demonstrators back to Selma in her car, when she was chased by Ku Klux Klansmen who shot her twice in the face. Her death was one of several caused by violence during the civil rights movement and a potent reminder of the risk of participation.

FROM CIVIL RIGHTS
TO HUMAN RIGHTS

FOLLOWING THE Selma-to-Montgomery march, Congress passed the Voting Rights Act, signed into law by President Johnson on August 6, 1965. As legal segregation ended, civil rights activists shifted their focus to the broader issues of the quality of education and health care, equality of job opportunities, and fair housing practices, not only in the South but throughout the United States. The struggle to end poverty and discrimination continues today. The same drive that motivated demonstrators to attain civil rights now moves them to demand human rights, not only for African Americans but for people throughout the world.

Women continue to play leading roles: Marian Wright Edelman, for example, founded and directs the Children's Defense Fund to lobby for child welfare; Myrlie Evers-Williams chaired the NAACP board from 1995 to 1998; and Eleanor Holmes Norton has served as a representative to Congress from the District of Columbia since 1990. These women already had a record of involvement and achievement in the civil rights movement of the 1950s and 1960s. For them, and for the many other women who participated, the movement proved to be not only a challenge, but an opportunity—to demonstrate their commitment to justice and equality; to share their support and strength; to take pride in themselves; to defy and reject violence; and ultimately, to change their history and the history of the United States. ■

■ *From the mid-1950s, Myrlie Evers-Williams (b. 1933) worked side by side with her husband, Medgar Evers, field secretary of the Mississippi NAACP. When he was murdered in 1963, she continued to speak in the organization's behalf. Here, Evers-Williams (on couch) is being comforted by several women after Evers' death.*
PHOTOGRAPH © BETTMAN/CORBIS

■ *Eleanor Holmes Norton (b. 1937) worked with CORE and SNCC and, as a young attorney, helped to write the brief used to argue on behalf of seating MFDP candidates at the 1964 Democratic National Convention. In 1977, she became the first woman to chair the Equal Employment Opportunity Commission.*

PHOTOGRAPH BY RHODA BEAR, COURTESY US CONGRESS

FOR FURTHER READING

Clark, Septima. *Ready from Within: Septima Clark and the Civil Rights Movement.* Cynthia Stokes Brown, ed. Navarro, CA: Wild Trees Press, 1986.

Clark, Septima, with LeGette Blythe. *Echo in My Soul.* New York: Dutton, 1962.

Crawford, Vicki L., Jacqueline Anne Rouse, and Barbara Woods, eds. *Women in the Civil Rights Movement: Trailblazers and Torchbearers, 1941–1965.* Brooklyn, NY: Carlson Publishing, 1990.

Curry, Constance, et al., *Deep in Our Hearts: Nine White Women in the Freedom Movement.* Athens: University of Georgia Press, 2000.

Hine, Darlene Clark, Elsa Barkley Brown, and Rosalyn Terborg-Penn, eds. *Black Women in America: An Historical Encyclopedia.* Two volumes. Bloomington: Indiana University Press, 1993.

Lanker, Brian. *I Dream a World: Portraits of Black Women Who Changed America.* New York: Stewart, Tabori & Chang, 1989.

Olson, Lynne. *Freedom's Daughters: The Unsung Heroines of the Civil Rights Movement from 1830 to 1970.* New York: Scribner, 2001.

Raines, Howell, ed. *My Soul Is Rested: Movement Days in the Deep South Remembered.* New York: Penguin Books, 1983.

Robinson, Jo Ann Gibson. *The Montgomery Bus Boycott and the Women Who Started It: The Memoir of Jo Ann Gibson Robinson.* David J. Garrow, ed. Knoxville: University of Tennessee Press, 1987.

Williams, Juan. *Eyes on the Prize: America's Civil Rights Years, 1954–1965.* New York: Penguin Books, 1988.

ACKNOWLEDGMENTS

The author wishes to acknowledge Karen Berman for her help in securing Ida Berman's photograph of Septima Clark and Michael Schulman of Magnum Photos for his assistance with the photographs by Danny Lyon. Special thanks go to Amy Pastan, series editor, who provided invaluable additional research and support.

IMAGES

Reproduction numbers, when available, are given for all items in the collections of the Library of Congress. Unless otherwise noted, Library of Congress images are from the Prints and Photographs Division. To order reproductions, note the LC-number provided with the image; where no number exists, note the Library division and the title of the item. Direct your request to:

The Library of Congress
Photoduplication Service
Washington DC 20540-4570
(202) 707-5640; www.loc.gov